CW01073027

Reading and writing
Tamzin Thompson

Unit	Structures	Vocabulary	Skills
1 Use your imagination page 4	Imperatives Sequencing words: *First ..., Next ...*	Making things: *imagination, carve, sculpture,* etc.	📖 *How to make a mask* (instructions) ✏ Instructions
2 Working with animals page 8	Modals: *need to ..., mustn't ..., have to ...*	Describing jobs: *train (v), recognize, hope,* etc.	📖 *I would like to be a vet* (description of a job) ✏ A job I would like to have
3 Extreme weather page 12	Comparative and superlative of adjectives Order of adjectives	Describing weather conditions: *thermometer, sunfall, temperature,* etc.	📖 *Cherrapunji* (description of a place) ✏ A description of Valdez
4 Unusual houses page 16	*have got: It's only got one room.* Adjectives: *extremely, very, quite, not very*	Unusual places: *upside down, tourist attraction, unlike,* etc.	📖 *An interesting house* (description of a house) ✏ An unusual building
5 Life in the future page 20	*will / won't / think / imagine* for predictions: *There will be ..., I think ...*	Inventions and technology: *3D, network, wire,* etc.	📖 *A day in my life in 2020* (prediction) ✏ Everyday life in the future
6 Clever creatures page 24	*can* infinitive of purpose	Animals: *nest, creature, crow,* etc.	📖 *Meet the octopus* (paragraphs with topic sentences) ✏ Blue whales
7 A helping hand page 28	Making suggestions: *Why not ..., Perhaps you could ...*	People in need: *famine, poverty, disaster,* etc.	📖 *Girls raise money for hospital* (news report) ✏ A news report
8 Sweet and tasty page 32	First conditional: *Chocolate will give you energy if you are tired.*	Recipes and cooking: *bitter, tasty, melt,* etc.	📖 *Colourful cupcakes* (recipe) ✏ A recipe
9 Journeys into space page 36	Wh- questions	Space exploration: *development, cosmonaut, spacecraft,* etc.	📖 *Space Quiz* (questions and answers) ✏ Questions for a quiz
10 It's time for a story page 40	Past simple Adjectives in stories	Verbs in stories: *bury, slip, greet,* etc.	📖 *A Lucky Day* (story) ✏ A story
11 Winners page 44	The passive Syllables and rhyming words	Competitions: *award, ceremony, compete,* etc.	📖 *The Winner* (poem) ✏ A poem
12 Remarkable women page 48	Time linkers: *When ..., By the time ..., Finally ...*	Stories from the past: *remarkable, fiction, peace,* etc.	📖 *Helen Keller* (life story) ✏ A life story
More words page 52		Six extra words for each unit	

OXFORD
UNIVERSITY PRESS

Teaching notes

The *Oxford Primary Skills* series is designed to be used alongside your main coursebook, to further develop reading and writing skills. The series uses a balance of familiar and new language in a range of contexts.

Levels 5 and 6 are made up of twelve teaching units, to be used in order. The texts progress in difficulty from unit to unit, introducing new vocabulary and structures and developing writing skills. The grammar and vocabulary syllabus is designed to be consistent with what the children are learning in their main coursebook.

Reading

The series introduces children to different types of written English, using a variety of texts. Children will be motivated when they find that they can read and understand 'real' text types such as, newspaper reports, recipes or traditional tales – all written in language appropriate to their stage of learning. Through doing various types of comprehension activities, children will develop the skills of reading and listening for gist and detail, which are essential for all-round communicative competence. Finally, by doing vocabulary exercises and becoming competent dictionary users, children will develop skills that will enable them to approach new words and texts with confidence.

Writing

In the *Writing* section of each unit, children practise and revise writing subskills such as topic sentences and time linkers. They will also learn how to improve their writing by using language appropriate to the context. Children are given a variety of writing tasks, which will develop their ability to use the language more flexibly. Their writing confidence will develop as they produce a wide range of texts, including instructions, questions for a quiz and a poem.

More words

The *More words* section at the back of the book presents supplementary vocabulary which children can use in their writing tasks. Some of these words will be new; others are presented as revision. It is to be stressed that these words are optional and it is perfectly possible to complete the course without using this additional section.

Tour of a unit

The twelve units cover topics that children are likely to meet in their main English coursebook or in other school subjects. Each unit follows the same structure:

Reading

Before reading

Each unit begins with open class discussion questions. These questions are designed to focus children on the unit topic. They help children to draw on their own understanding of the topic, and from this to make predictions about the content of the text.

It may be useful to pre-teach a few words in the text which could cause special problems, but do not try to solve every difficulty beforehand. Guessing the sense of unknown words is an important part of developing reading skills.

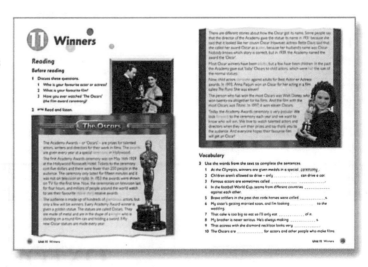

Read and listen

Each text is recorded on the Teacher's CD. Play the recording as children follow in their books. Listening to the reading text and reading silently will develop children's ability to read for gist. It is not important for them to understand every word at this point. Reading without interruption is important if they are to gain a general understanding of the text. After reading and listening, ask a few simple comprehension questions to ensure children understand the gist.

Vocabulary

In the vocabulary exercise that follows the *Reading* section, children choose highlighted words from the text to complete the sentences or match to the definitions. Presenting new vocabulary in context, and encouraging children to look up the definitions in their dictionaries, develops children's confidence and competence as independent readers.

Reading comprehension

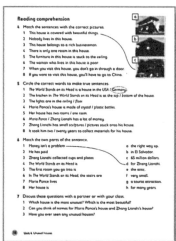

The exercises in the *Reading comprehension* section will allow you to monitor children's understanding of the text, both in general and in detail. Make sure that children understand the task. Answer one or two of the questions with the class if you feel this is necessary, then let the children finish the exercise on their own. The exercises could also be given as homework, giving children the opportunity to re-read the text at their own speed – an ideal way to build on their work in class.

The last exercise on the *Reading comprehension* page is intended to promote classroom discussion and introduce related topics. Encourage children to express their own ideas and opinions. They could also discuss the questions at home with their families in their own language, then report their findings back to the class in English.

Writing

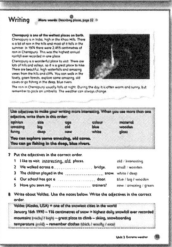

The *Writing* page begins with a short text which children can use as a model for their own writing. Children should read the text through, focusing on gaining a general understanding. Again you can ask a few simple questions just to check comprehension. These texts do not present new or difficult vocabulary as they are designed to focus on writing sub-skills rather than vocabulary development.

Below each text are writing tips in preparation for the task that will conclude the unit. They cover a variety of writing points: lexis, syntax, idiom and structure. Tell the children that you want them to make use of these tips in their own writing. Use the exercise which follows the writing tips for practice and reinforcement. Children should complete these exercises on their own, but do feedback as a class before they move on to the writing task.

Read the instructions for the final writing activity with the children, to be sure that everyone understands what they have to do. Less confident writers can stay close to the model text, copying its structure while substituting vocabulary; other children may be able to write more independently. Children who are progressing well with their writing may be encouraged to use the optional *More words* section at the back of the book, which provides additional vocabulary that can be used in the writing task.

For more extensive teaching notes and answer key, go to www.oup.com/elt/teachersclub/young_learners

1 Use your imagination

Reading

Before reading

1 Look at the photos and discuss these questions.

   1 Have you ever seen works of art like these? Where?

   2 What do you think they are made of?

   3 How do you think they are made?

2 –01– Read and listen.

Amazing sculptures

"You can make anything out of ice," says Ian Foster. Ian is an ice sculptor. He carves animals, buildings and trees – all out of ice. The biggest ice sculpture he ever made was an entire castle.

Each sculpture begins with a piece of paper, a pencil and Ian's imagination. He makes drawings of the sculpture and imagines it from the front and back and from every side. Once he is happy with his idea, he starts to work with his tools on a big block of ice.

"I have to wear a thick coat and a fur hat to work, even when it's hot outside. The temperature in the studio is always close to freezing. Otherwise the sculpture would melt. It's like working in a big fridge."

Most of the sculptures are made for special occasions: weddings, town festivals or parties in big companies. The sculptures are taken to the party in refrigerated vans. Once they are taken out of the van and put on show, they begin to melt. However, the biggest sculptures will last for many hours before they turn into water.

Does Ian feel sad when his sculptures melt? "Not really," he says, "because I am already thinking about the next sculpture."

Melting ice is not a problem for Mike Evans. He is a sand sculptor.

Mike started making sand sculptures 24 years ago, and for the last 16 years sand sculpture has been his full-time job. He works with a team of sculptors. They travel all over the world to make sand art for festivals, shows, museums, zoos, shopping centres and big companies.

The team has made hundreds of sculptures, from small statues to a huge palace for a hundred people to have dinner inside. They never make the same sculpture twice. The team has won lots of prizes for their art. They also teach people how to make sand sculptures.

1 To make a sand sculpture, you need a wooden frame. First, fill the frame with sand, then use water to wet the sand. Press the sand down into the frame until the sand is hard.

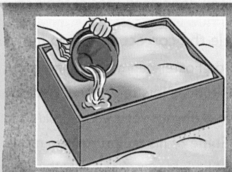

2 Then remove the frame and start to carve the sand sculpture. Start at the top of the sculpture. You can use gardening tools, a stick and an ordinary knife to carve the sand.

Vocabulary

3 Use the words from the text to complete the sentences.

1 Artists use their <u>imagination</u> to make beautiful things.

2 A _____ is an artist who carves things out of stone.

3 An ice sculptor _____ amazing things out of ice.

4 Ice sculptors start their sculptures with a big _____ of ice.

5 To make a big sand sculpture, you need a wooden _____.

6 You must _____ the green button to turn on the computer.

7 If you leave ice cream in a warm room, it will _____.

8 Big _____ usually have their offices in large cities.

9 Birthdays, weddings and festivals are all special _____.

10 My mum works in an office three days a week. She doesn't want a _____ job.

Reading comprehension

4 Write *True* or *False*.

1 Ian Foster makes sculptures out of ice.   <u>True</u>

2 He wears a T-shirt at work because it's hot.   _____

3 His sculptures begin to melt when they are put on show.   _____

4 Ian is very sad when his sculptures melt.   _____

5 Mike Evans started making sand sculptures last year.   _____

6 His team makes sand sculptures all over the world.   _____

7 They make the same sculptures all the time.   _____

8 You don't need special tools to make a sand sculpture.   _____

5 Circle the correct words to make true sentences.

1 Ian Foster can make animals out of *paper* / *ice.*

2 He does lots of *drawings* / *paintings* before he makes a sculpture.

3 It is always very *warm* / *cold* in Ian's studio.

4 Some of his sculptures are made for parties in big *shops* / *companies.*

5 Mike Evans makes *sculptures* / *pictures* out of sand.

6 He's been making sand sculptures for *24* / *16* years.

7 The team has won prizes *twice* / *lots of times.*

8 If you make a sand sculpture, use *a frame* / *gardening tools* to carve the sand.

6 Write short answers.

1 Does Ian Foster make ice sculptures of animals?   <u>Yes, he does.</u>

2 Has he ever made a castle out of ice?   _____

3 Do ice sculptures last many days?   _____

4 Is sand sculpture Mike Evans' hobby?   _____

5 Does Mike work with other sculptors?   _____

6 Do we know how many sculptors work with Mike?   _____

7 Can you use an ordinary knife to make a sand sculpture?   _____

8 Do you need to make the sand wet when you make a
sand sculpture?   _____

7 Discuss these questions with a partner or with your class.

1 Would you like to be an ice sculptor? Why? / Why not?

2 Imagine you are going to make a sculpture. What would you make?

3 Do you like making things? What tools do you use?

Writing

More words: Giving instructions, page 52

How to make a mask

You need ...

| a balloon | old newspapers | paste | paint | paintbrush | scissors |

1 First, blow up a balloon, then tie the top. Put the balloon on a cup while you work on it.

2 Next, cut the newspaper into long strips. Then put the pieces of newspaper in the paste.

3 Cover half of the balloon with the wet strips of newspaper. When you have added one layer of newspaper, use cardboard to make a nose and ears. Then cover the mask with more layers of newspaper.

4 When your mask has dried, pop the balloon. Use scissors to cut holes in the mask for your eyes and mouth. Finally, paint your mask.

When you write instructions for making something ...
- Give a list of what you need.
- Use imperatives to tell people what to do:
  blow up / tie / put / cut
- Use sequencing words for each step:
  first / next / then / finally
- Use *to* when you explain what we do with something:
  Use scissors to cut holes in the mask.
- Use *with* when you suggest what to use:
  Cover the balloon with strips of newspaper.

---

8 Complete the sentences. Use *to* or *with*.

  1 Find some old newspaper _to_ cover the table.

  2 Fill a cup _____ water.

  3 You can use the water _____ wet your paintbrush.

  4 Use your paintbrush _____ paint the card.

  5 You can decorate the card _____ stickers or pictures.

9 Write instructions for making something, for example, a picture frame, a hat or a fan, or write about something you have made in the past.

Reading

Before reading

1 Discuss these questions.

1 What do you know about sharks?

2 Are you afraid of sharks?

3 Do you think sharks are clever animals?

2 ⊷02⊶ Read and listen.

Sarah Turner

Sarah Turner has an unusual job.
She trains sharks at the Sea Life Centre.
We asked Sarah a few questions to find out more about her job.

Why did you become a shark trainer?

I've always loved sharks. They're amazing creatures and they're very clever. Lots of people are scared of them, of course. I want to learn more about them so that I can teach people not to be scared.

What do you do at work?

I usually feed, study and train the sharks here at the Sea Life Centre. The sharks live in huge tanks. I also study sharks in their natural habitat. You need to be brave to dive with a video camera to film the sharks in the sea!

How do you train the sharks at the Sea Life Centre?

We teach them to touch a special button to get food. There is a different button for every species of shark here. Every button is a different colour and has a different pattern on it. The sharks learn to recognize their button and press it with their noses when they are hungry. We move the buttons around the tank so that the sharks learn to follow them.

What does this teach us about sharks?

Many things. It tells us that sharks can understand and remember. They understand that one button means "food", although it doesn't look like food. And when we put the button in a different place, they still remember it.

Why do you train the sharks?

Sharks usually stay in groups. We want to teach the sharks to come to special places so that we can study them and check their health. We start by teaching them to come to different places to get food. We have to teach them one thing at a time. Sharks get scared when you try to do lots of things at once.

What other things have you learnt about sharks?

I've learnt a lot about their eating habits and routines. I've also learnt that all sharks have different personalities. One of the young sharks here likes to chase the bigger sharks. She also likes to play with her food. I hope my work will teach people that sharks are not monsters. They are often clever, funny creatures.

Vocabulary

3   Match the words from the text to the definitions.

1   recognize   (verb) to know again something that you have seen before
2   _____   (verb) to keep something in your memory
3   _____   (verb) to know what something means or why something happens
4   _____   (verb) to want something to happen
5   _____   (verb) to teach a person or an animal to do something
6   _____   (noun) a group of animals that are the same
7   _____   (noun) the natural place where an animal lives
8   _____   (noun) a large container that holds liquid
9   _____   (noun) shapes and colours on something
10 _____   (noun) things that a person or animal does often

Reading comprehension

4 Write *True* or *False*.

1 Sarah works in a fish shop.   <u>False</u>

2 Sarah doesn't want people to be scared of sharks.   _____

3 The sharks learn to touch a button to get food.   _____

4 The sharks learn to move the button around the tank.   _____

5 The sharks think that the buttons are food.   _____

6 The sharks learn that one button means "food".   _____

7 Sarah has learnt that all sharks have different personalities.   _____

8 Sarah's job has taught her that sharks are monsters.   _____

5 Match the two parts of the sentences.

1 Sarah's job is   a   sharks in the sea.

2 She became a shark trainer because   b   the older sharks.

3 The sharks live   c   she's always loved sharks.

4 Sometimes Sarah films   d   one thing at a time.

5 The sharks don't forget the food button   e   very unusual.

6 Sarah teaches the sharks   f   clever and funny.

7 One young shark chases   g   in a big tank.

8 Sharks can be   h   when Sarah moves it.

6 Complete the facts. Write one word in each gap.

1 Sarah <u>works</u> at the Sea Life Centre.

2 She wants to learn more about _____.

3 Sarah sometimes _____ in the sea with a video camera.

4 She teaches the sharks to press _____ with their noses.

5 When the sharks press the correct button, Sarah gives them _____.

6 Sarah wants to check the sharks' _____.

7 Sharks _____ like doing lots of things at once.

8 There is one _____ shark that likes to play with her food.

7 Discuss these questions with a partner or with your class.

1 Do you think Sarah Turner has a good job? Why or why not?

2 Why are some people scared of sharks?

3 Has the text taught you anything new about sharks? What was the most interesting thing you learnt?

Writing

More words: Personalities, page 52

Q: What job would you like to have? Why?

I think I'd like to be a vet. One reason is that a vet sees many different animals with different problems, so the job isn't boring. Another reason is that it's good to help sick animals. You know that you are doing a useful job and helping animals and their owners.

You have to know about animals and their health. You need to be good at science, especially biology. You need to be kind and friendly. You mustn't be afraid of dogs or big animals.

It's important to study every animal carefully, so that you can help them.

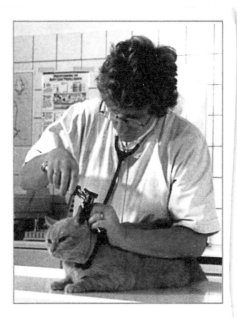

When you answer the question *Why?* you may want to give a long answer. Split up your answer:

One reason is that ... Another reason is that ...

When you describe a job, think about what someone needs to be like to do the job well:

You need to be calm and patient. You mustn't be afraid of dogs.

Also think about what someone should know:

You have to know about animals and their health.

8   Match and make sentences.

1   I think that being — a   that all animals have different personalities.

2   One reason is — b   afraid of dangerous animals.

3   You have to know about — c   a zoo keeper is an interesting job.

4   You need to be — d   to know all the animals and their personalities.

5   You mustn't be — e   animals and their eating habits.

6   It's important — f   clever and patient.

9   Write about the job you would like to have. Why would you like this job? Use these words and phrases.

I think I'd like to be a ...	*One reason is that ...*	*Another reason is that ...*
You have to know about ...	*You need to be ...*	*You mustn't be ...*

③ Extreme weather

Reading

Before reading

1 Look at the photos. Discuss these questions.

  1 Where do you think these places are?

  2 What do you think the weather is like in these places?

  3 Would you like to visit these places? Why or why not?

2 ◦03◦ Read and listen.

The hottest place on Earth

On September 13th 1922, scientists in El Azizia in Libya recorded a temperature of 57.8°C. This is the hottest temperature ever recorded.

The temperature changes all the time. Summer is hotter than winter, and days are usually warmer than nights. If we want to know the correct temperature, we look at a thermometer. Thermometers show us the temperature in degrees. For example, if the temperature is 30 degrees Celsius (30°C), it is a nice, warm day. However, 40°C is hot and uncomfortable.

If the temperature is 5°C, it is a cold day. Water freezes at 0°C, but in very cold places the temperature falls below zero. Very cold temperatures are measured in negative numbers, for example, minus five degrees Celsius (−5°C).

El Azizia is near the Sahara Desert. Scientists believe that the temperature in the desert is even hotter than the temperature in El Azizia, but there are no weather stations in the desert to record the temperature.

Libya is one of the hottest places in the world because a hot, sandy wind blows across the country in the spring and autumn. The wind can raise the temperature by 20°C in just a couple of hours. Also, there is very little water in the desert and it hardly ever rains. In some parts of Libya, ten years can pass without rain. In Uweinat on the border between Libya and Egypt, the last rain was recorded in 1998.

... and the coldest place

In 1983, Russian scientists working in Antarctica recorded a temperature of −89°C. This is the coldest temperature ever recorded.

Antarctica is colder than the Arctic because the snow surface in Antarctica is higher than in the Arctic. Also, the North Pole is in the middle of the Arctic Ocean. Although most of the sea is frozen, it is not as cold as the South Pole in Antarctica. Under the snow in Antarctica there is land, not ocean. Land can get colder than a frozen sea, so Antarctica is colder than the Arctic.

Antarctica is also the driest continent on Earth. It gets less than ten centimetres of rain every year. This means that Antarctica is a desert, because a desert is a place where there is less than 25.4 centimetres of rain every year. There is a lot of water in Antarctica, but it is all frozen in huge ice sheets. However, you can still get sunburn in Antarctica, because the snow reflects the sun.

Vocabulary

3 Use the words from the text to complete the sentences.

1 El Paso is on the _border_ between the United States and Mexico.

2 In El Paso it _____ ever rains in the summer.

3 In winter in Russia, the temperature is often below _____.

4 One hundred degrees _____ is written as 100°C.

5 The _____ on the moon is about 107°C in the day.

6 At night, the temperature on the moon falls to about −153°C. That's a difference of 260 _____.

7 Scientists in Libya _____ a temperature of 57.8°C in 1922.

8 In the desert, the temperature can change a lot in a _____ of hours.

9 If you want to know the temperature, look at a _____.

10 You will get _____ if you lie in the sun for too long.

Reading comprehension

4 Write *Libya* or *Antarctica*.

1 The South Pole is in <u>Antarctica</u>.

2 All the water in _____ is frozen.

3 Scientists recorded a temperature of 57.8°C in _____.

4 On the border between _____ and Egypt it hardly ever rains.

5 The Arctic is warmer than _____.

6 _____ is one of the hottest countries in the world.

7 _____ is the driest continent in the world.

8 A hot wind blows across _____ for some of the year.

5 Circle the correct words to make true sentences.

1 We use *scientists* / (thermometers) to show us the temperature.

2 A temperature of *40°C* / *20°C* isn't very comfortable.

3 When the temperature falls below *zero* / *30°C*, the weather is very cold.

4 El Azizia is in *Russia* / *Libya*.

5 Scientists *believe* / *don't believe* that some places are hotter than El Azizia.

6 In Libya it's *hot* / *cold* and windy in the autumn.

7 Russian scientists in *Antarctica* / *the Arctic* recorded the coldest temperature ever.

8 There *is lots of* / *isn't much* rain in Antarctica.

6 Answer the questions.

1 What does *C* mean in *30°C*?   <u>Celsius</u>

2 What are measured in negative numbers?   _____

3 Are there any weather stations in the desert?   _____

4 When was the last rain recorded in Uweinat?   _____

5 What was the coldest temperature ever recorded?   _____

6 What is in the middle of the Arctic Ocean?   _____

7 What is under the snow in Antarctica?   _____

8 How much rain does Antarctica get?   _____

7 Discuss these questions with a partner or with your class.

1 What clothes do you wear on hot days and on cold days?

2 What is the hottest place you have been to? What is the coldest place?

3 How many hot countries can you name? How many cold countries?

4 Would you prefer to live in a very hot or a very cold country?

Writing

More words: Describing places, page 52

Cherrapunji is one of the wettest places on Earth.
Cherrapunji is in India, high in the Khasi Hills. There is a lot of rain in the hills and most of it falls in the summer. In 1974 there were 2,455 centimetres of rain in Cherrapunji. This was the highest annual rainfall ever recorded in one place.

Cherrapunji is a wonderful place to visit. There are lots of hills and valleys, so it is a great place to hike. There are beautiful, high waterfalls and amazing views from the hills and cliffs. You can walk in the lovely, green forests, explore some amazing, old caves or go fishing in the deep, blue rivers.

The rain in Cherrapunji usually falls at night. During the day it is often warm and sunny, but remember to pack an umbrella. The weather can always change.

Use adjectives to make your writing more interesting. When you use more than one adjective, write them in this order:

opinion	size	age	colour	material
amazing	big	old	blue	wooden
funny	deep	new	white	glass

You can explore some amazing, old caves.
You can go fishing in the deep, blue rivers.

---

7 Put the adjectives in the correct order.

1 I like to visit _interesting, old_ places.   old / interesting

2 We walked across a _____ bridge.   small / wooden

3 The children played in the _____ snow.   white / deep

4 Our school has got a _____ door.   blue / big / wooden

5 Have you seen my _____ trainers?   new / amazing / green

8 Write about Valdez. Use the notes below. Write the adjectives in the correct order.

> Valdez (Alaska, USA) = one of the snowiest cities in the world
>
> January 16th 1990 – 116 centimetres of snow = highest daily snowfall ever recorded
>
> mountains (rocky / high) – great place to climb – skiing, snowboarding
>
> temperature (cold) – remember clothes (thick / woolly / nice)

4 Unusual houses

Reading

Before reading

1 Discuss these questions.

   1   Do you live in a house or a flat?

   2   How many rooms are there? What are they?

   3   Look at the picture. Does this look like your home? What's different?

2 Read and listen.

All around the world, houses look similar – doors, windows, a roof – but here are three houses that are very unusual and would look out of place in any country!

Welcome to a home with a difference. In most ways, this is a normal house. It's quite big. There's a living room, a kitchen, a bathroom and three bedrooms. But every week hundreds of people come to see this house.

What's unusual about it? It's upside down! You walk in through a window and the first room you come to is the attic. When you go upstairs to the bedrooms, there are more surprises. Look up and you'll see beds and wardrobes stuck to the ceiling. Look down and you'll see lights that come up from the floor.

At the top of the house there's a living room and a kitchen. Where's the sofa? Where's the cooker? They're on the ceiling, of course. Everything in this house is upside down. Only the stairs are the right way up, because visitors have to use them.

The house is a favourite tourist attraction, but nobody lives there. That would be impossible. Nobody could sleep upside down in a bed that's stuck to the ceiling.

This strange house is in Germany. Its name is unusual too. The house is called *The World Stands on its Head*.

Here's a more normal house. Firstly, it's the right way up. Secondly, the person who built it really lives there. However, the unusual thing about this house is that it's made of plastic bottles.

Maria Ponce's house is in a village in El Salvador in Central America. She didn't have enough money to build a normal house, so she collected empty plastic bottles and made a house with them. It took Maria nearly two years to collect the bottles and build her house and she is proud of it. It's only got one room but Maria hopes to build another room one day.

Zhang Lianzhi's house in north China is bigger than Maria Ponce's. However, like Maria, he has used his imagination to make a house that is unlike any other. His house is covered with pieces of beautiful cups and plates which he collected for more than twenty years. He has also stuck small sculptures onto his house, and pieces of coloured crystal. All these beautiful things have cost Zhang 65 million dollars. Fortunately, Zhang is a rich businessman, so money isn't a problem for him.

Vocabulary

3 Match the words from the text to the definitions.

1 <u>tourist attraction</u>   *(noun)* something that tourists want to visit
2 _____ *(adjective)* with the top part at the bottom; these words are upside down
3 _____ *(adjective)* in the correct position; not upside down
4 _____ *(adjective)* usual and ordinary; not different
5 _____ *(adjective)* not usual; strange or different
6 _____ *(noun)* the top part of a room
7 _____ *(noun)* the room or space under the roof of a house
8 _____ *(noun)* a kind of rock that looks like glass
9 _____ *(adjective)* different from
10 _____ *(adjective)* something you can't do

Reading comprehension

4 Match the sentences with the correct pictures.

1   This house is covered with beautiful things.
2   Nobody lives in this house.
3   This house belongs to a rich businessman.
4   There is only one room in this house.
5   The furniture in this house is stuck to the ceiling.
6   The woman who lives in this house is poor.
7   When you visit this house, you don't go in through a door.
8   If you want to visit this house, you'll have to go to China.

5 Circle the correct words to make true sentences.

1   *The World Stands on its Head* is a house in *the USA* / *Germany.*
2   The kitchen in *The World Stands on its Head* is at the *top* / *bottom* of the house.
3   The lights are in the *ceiling* / *floor.*
4   Maria Ponce's house is made of *crystal* / *plastic bottles.*
5   Her house has *two rooms* / *one room.*
6   *Maria Ponce* / *Zhang Lianzhi* has a lot of money.
7   Zhang Lianzhi has small *sculptures* / *pictures* stuck onto his house.
8   It took him *two* / *twenty* years to collect materials for his house.

6 Match the two parts of the sentence.

1   Money isn't a problem
2   He has paid
3   Zhang Lianzhi collected cups and plates
4   *The World Stands on its Head* is
5   The first room you go into is
6   In *The World Stands on its Head*, the stairs are
7   Maria Ponce lives
8   Her house is

a   the right way up.
b   in El Salvador.
c   65 million dollars.
d   for Zhang Lianzhi.
e   the attic.
f   very small.
g   a tourist attraction.
h   for many years.

7 Discuss these questions with a partner or with your class.

1   Which house is the most unusual? Which is the most beautiful?
2   Can you think of names for Maria Ponce's house and Zhang Lianzhi's house?
3   Have you ever seen any unusual houses?

Writing

More words: Buildings, page 53

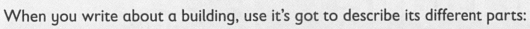

An interesting house

When we visit my uncle and aunt in the countryside, we pass a very unusual house. It's quite big and very pretty, but the strange thing about this house is that it's got grass on the roof. It looks like a garden on top of the house.

Dad saw an article about this house in the newspaper. It's a good idea to put soil and grass on the roof because it saves energy and it is extremely good for the environment. The soil keeps the house quite warm in winter. In summer, it feels quite cool inside.

I would love to live in this house. It's not very close to the town, but it's interesting and fun, and we could play on the roof!

When you write about a building, use it's got to describe its different parts:

It's got a red door.   It's got grass on the roof.   It's only got one room.

Use extremely, very, quite and not very to describe the house:

It's very big.   It's quite big.

Say why the building is interesting:

The unusual / strange thing about this building is that ...

8 Complete the sentences using *extremely, very, quite* and *not very*.

1 Mount Everest is _____ high.

2 My building's got eight floors. It's _____ tall.

3 Sardines _____ big fish– they are only about 10 cm long.

4 Blue whales are _____ big – they can be up to 27 metres long.

5 Summer in England is _____ warm.

6 It is usually _____ hot in Antarctica.

9 Write about an unusual house or building that you have seen.

Describe its size and appearance. Use *extremely, very, quite* or *not very*.

Write about different parts of the building. Use *it's got*.

Say why it is unusual.

5 Life in the future

Reading

Before reading

1 Discuss these questions.

   1 How old will you be in 20 years? Think about your life then.

   2 Do you think computers, TVs and phones will be the same? How will they look?

   3 Do you think that we will all have robots in our homes?

2 ◄05► Read and listen.

Our future

In the next few decades, new inventions and discoveries will make huge changes to our lives. On these two pages, scientists give their predictions about life in the future.

Will there be schools in the future?

Yes, children will still go to school, but schools will be very different. There will still be teachers, but computers will teach some lessons. Some students will stay at home and learn in virtual classrooms. Virtual reality will give them an image of a classroom in three dimensions – or 3D. They will see their teacher and their friends, so they will feel like they are really at school.

Will computers understand what we say to them?

Computers will be more intelligent. They will understand what we say, what we think and how we feel. In the future, humans and computers will be part of a huge radio network. We will send messages from our brain to our computer and the computer will send messages straight to our brain, without using wires. When you want to learn something new, your computer will send the information straight to your brain.

What will clothes be like?

In a few years there will be clothes with soft TV screens in them. You will be able to change the pattern on your T-shirt. You will be able to show music videos on your clothes while you are dancing. Before long, there will be jackets with a soft watch on the sleeve.

Will we have robots to help us?

In the future, we will have lots of very clever robots called nanobots. Nanobots will be very small, but they will be everywhere. They will clean our homes, mend our clothes and make our meals.

Will there be televisions?

Televisions in the future will be different from televisions now. They will be much bigger and the pictures on the television won't be flat. They will all be in 3D. You will be able to walk into your favourite TV programme. It will happen all around you.

What about TV channels?

TV channels will be a thing of the past. People will choose TV programmes from a menu on their computer. In the future, TV programmes, films, music and books will all come to us through our computers. We will say to the computer, "I want to watch a funny film" or "I'd like to hear some dance music." The computer will understand us and choose the film or the music.

Vocabulary

3 Use the words from the text to complete the sentences.

1 There are many _predictions_ about our future.

2 A _____ is a tiny robot which will help people with the housework.

3 All the computers at our school are on the same _____.

4 When you click on the HELP icon, a _____ appears.

5 Your _____ is in your head. You use it to think.

6 There are ten years in a _____.

7 *SimCity* is a computer game. You can use it to create a _____ city.

8 Usually, a _____ attaches a computer to a printer.

9 The picture on a TV or computer is often called an _____.

10 "This TV programme isn't interesting. Let's try another _____."

Reading comprehension

4 Write *True* or *False*.

1 There won't be any schools in the future.   <u>False</u>

2 In some lessons, computers will teach the students.   _____

3 Some students will have lessons at home.   _____

4 We will have computers in our brains.   _____

5 Our brains will be connected to computers with wires.   _____

6 Some people will have TV screens on their clothes.   _____

7 There will be a lot more TV channels.   _____

8 We will be able to speak to our computers.   _____

5 Complete the facts. Write one word in each gap.

1 Sometimes students will learn in a virtual <u>classroom</u>.

2 Computers will _____ what people say.

3 People and _____ will be part of the same network.

4 Computers will send information straight to our _____.

5 Some _____ will have a watch on the sleeve.

6 Small _____ will help us in our homes.

7 There won't be any TV _____ in the future.

8 Your computer will _____ films and music for you.

6 Write short answers.

1 Will there be teachers in the future?   <u>Yes, there will.</u>

2 When students learn at home, will they see their friends?   _____

3 Will there be lots of wires on computers?   _____

4 Will computers know how people feel?   _____

5 Will all clothes be like they are now?   _____

6 Will there be little robots in people's houses?   _____

7 Will housework be easier?   _____

8 Will there be lots of TV channels?   _____

7 Discuss these questions with a partner or with your class.

1 Do you think these predictions will come true?

2 Do you think that virtual classrooms are better than real ones?

3 Do you think life will be better in the future? Why or why not?

Writing

More words: Inventions and technology, page 53

A day in my life in 2020

I imagine I will wake up early. I won't have an alarm clock. My computer will send a message to my brain to wake me up. I will have a shower and get dressed. For breakfast, I will tell my microwave how to cook my eggs. A robot will bring me tea.

I probably won't go to school. I think I'll have my lessons at home on my computer. The teacher's computer and all the students' computers will probably be part of the same network. Perhaps I'll go to a 3D cinema after lessons. I hope we'll drive there in a flying car!

Use think, imagine (that), and perhaps when you think something may happen but are not sure:

I think that we will all have robots in the future.
Perhaps I'll talk to my computer.

Use probably when you are more sure:

We will probably work at home with computers.

Use hope (that) when you want something to happen:

I hope I'll have a flying car.

---

8 Write predictions.

1 we / probably / have / tiny computers
    <u>We will probably have tiny computers.</u>

2 I think / people / go on holiday / in space

3 I imagine / scientists / invent / lots of new things

4 perhaps / students / have lessons / on the Internet

5 I hope / we / use / alternative energy

6 people / probably / travel / by spaceship

9 Write about a day in your life in 2050. Answer these questions.

Where will you live?	How will you travel?
What will you eat?	What will you do in your free time?

6 Clever creatures

Reading

Before reading

1 Discuss these questions.

   1 Which animals do you think are clever?

   2 Which do you think are the most clever: monkeys, birds or elephants?

2   06   Read and listen.

Which are the most intelligent animals in the world?

It's difficult to say, because different animals have different types of intelligence. For example, dolphins can speak a type of language. Also, some birds remember where they built nests and fly hundreds of miles to go back there. Or what about spiders? They make amazing webs, so maybe spiders are very intelligent too. Now let's meet three very clever creatures.

Koko the gorilla can talk.

She lives in California in the USA and she can use sign language to talk to people. Her teacher, Penny Patterson, has taught Koko more than 1,000 signs for different objects, actions and feelings.

Koko invents new signs when she sees new things. The first time she saw a duck, she used the sign for water and the sign for bird.

Penny believes that all gorillas can learn to use sign language, because they are a very intelligent species.

Crows are intelligent birds.
Betty, a crow who lives in England, is especially intelligent. The amazing thing about Betty is that she makes tools to get her food.

It's not unusual for crows to use twigs to pull food from holes in trees or in the ground. Betty can do more than that. She can pick up a piece of wire and bend it to make a hook. The hook is better than a straight piece of wire, because Betty can use it to get her food more easily.

What's more, she didn't make a hook just once, by accident. She has made hooks many times, while some scientists were watching her. Betty wasn't just lucky. She learnt and she remembered.

Now imagine an elephant that can paint. Sao is a 35-year-old elephant who lives in Thailand. When Sao was young, she worked in the forests. She used to pull up trees so that people could sell the wood. Then in the 1980s, companies stopped selling wood from the forests because there were not enough trees left.

Luckily, Sao has found a new job. She is a painter. She can hold a paintbrush with her trunk and paint beautiful pictures.

There are lots of elephant artists like Sao in Thailand. People can visit exhibitions and buy paintings by Sao and other amazing elephants. Sao's keepers are going to use the money from the paintings to help protect elephants.

Vocabulary

3 Match the words from the text to the definitions.

1 <u>by accident</u>   *(adverb)* by chance; not because you planned it
2 _____   *(verb)* to make something that was straight into a curved shape
3 _____   *(noun)* a curved piece of metal or plastic
4 _____   *(noun)* a black bird that makes a loud noise
5 _____   *(noun)* a bird that lives on or near water
6 _____   *(noun)* the place where a bird keeps its eggs
7 _____   *(noun)* a thin net that a spider makes to catch flies
8 _____   *(noun)* a language that uses hand movements, not speech
9 _____   *(noun)* a small, thin branch of tree
10 _____   *(noun)* an animal or bird; any living thing that is not a plant

Reading comprehension

4 Write *Koko, Betty* or *Sao.*

1 <u>Koko</u> is a gorilla.

2 _____ can paint beautiful pictures.

3 _____ knows lots of words in sign language.

4 _____ is a crow.

5 _____ used to work in the forests.

6 _____ bends pieces of wire.

7 _____ is thirty-five years old.

8 _____ can make hooks to get her food.

5 Circle the correct words to make true sentences.

1 Koko used two signs to say ⟨*duck*⟩/ '*bird*'.

2 Penny Patterson is Koko's *doctor / teacher*.

3 She says that gorillas are very *friendly / intelligent* animals.

4 Betty lives in *the UK / the USA*.

5 She made a hook when *visitors / scientists* were watching her.

6 Crows often use *grass / twigs* to get their food.

7 Sao uses her *trunk / mouth* to hold the brush.

8 She *is not / is* the only elephant in the world that can paint.

6 Answer the questions.

1 What clever thing can spiders do? <u>make a web</u>

2 Which animal in the text lives in California? _____

3 What are Betty's hooks made of? _____

4 Why does she make them? _____

5 Where does Sao live? _____

6 What job did Sao do in the forests? _____

7 Why did she change her job? _____

8 Why do her keepers sell her paintings? _____

7 Discuss these questions with a partner or with the class.

1 Which is the cleverest animal: Koko, Betty or Sao?

2 Think of other clever animals. What amazing things can they do?

3 Describe an animal and what it can do. Don't say what the animal is. Ask your friends to guess.

Writing

More words: Sea life, page 54

Meet the octopus:
the intelligent invertebrate

Octopuses are unusual and interesting creatures. They look strange because they have eight legs and because they are invertebrates. This means that they have no back bones.

Octopuses are the most intelligent invertebrates. They can open jars and bottles to get food. Parts of an octopus's brain are in its legs so its legs can actually think!

Octopuses can remember things. When an octopus has solved a problem once, it remembers and does the same thing another day. They can remember different shapes and patterns. We know this because scientists have studied octopuses for a long time.

We use topic sentences to introduce information in a piece of writing. Topic sentences go at the beginning of a paragraph:

Octopuses are the most intelligent invertebrates. Octopuses can remember things.

---

8 Match the topic sentences to the paragraphs.

1 Octopuses are invertebrates.   **3 Octopuses like to play.**

2 Octopuses learn with no help.

a   Young octopuses don't stay with their parents so they don't learn from them. They don't have teachers: they teach themselves!

b   Because they have no bones in their bodies, octopuses can hide in small places between rocks.

c   Sometimes octopuses throw things and catch them. They are like children playing with a ball.

9 Write about blue whales. Use the topic sentences (a to c) and the notes.

---

a) Blue whales are the biggest animals in the world.
b) They live in small groups.   c) They are not dangerous to humans.

– more than 30 metres long   – can use sounds to talk

– bigger than dinosaurs   – only eat small sea creatures

– usually two or three whales in a group   – intelligent and gentle

---

7 A helping hand

Reading

Before reading

1 Discuss these questions.

   1 Do you ever help people who are poor?

   2 How can we help them?

   3 What other people might need help? Think about your own country and others.

2 🔊07 Read and listen.

What is Oxfam?

Oxfam is a charity that helps people all over the world. Oxfam started in Oxford in 1942, when a group of people decided to help victims of famine. The group was called the Oxford Committee for Famine Relief, but the name soon became Oxfam. Today, Oxfam works in more than 70 countries around the world to make people's lives better.

What does Oxfam do?

Oxfam helps people who are poor, hungry or in trouble. Oxfam sends helpers to different countries to work with local people and try to find solutions to poverty and other problems. Oxfam trains health workers, builds schools, gives food and shelter and makes sure that people have clean water to drink. Oxfam also helps people in natural disasters, like floods or hurricanes.

What can you do?

Here are some imple ways you can help.

- **Raise money for Oxfam**

There are lots of fun ways to raise money. Why not organize a concert or a sporting event at your school and sell tickets? Or perhaps you could make cakes and sweets and sell them to people.

- **Give an Oxfam gift**

Are you looking for a special gift for a friend? When you buy an Oxfam gift, your friend will get a card and Oxfam will send a gift to a poor country. The gift can be something like a meal, clean water, a tree or a goat. Sometimes a few friends put their money together to buy a big gift, like a water tank to give clean water to a whole village.

- **Read and learn**

It is important to learn about what is happening in the world. Read newspapers and use the Internet to learn more about the world we live in. There are lots of ideas for school on the Oxfam website, with information about disasters, famine, clean water and environmental subjects. When you know about the problems in the world, you can start to look for solutions.

- **Spread the word**

Your friends and family care about what you think, so tell them your ideas. What do you want to change in the world? How do you think we can make that change? Talking to people is the first step to making things happen. You can find people with the same opinions and ideas and work together to make your world a better place.

Vocabulary

3 Use the words from the text to complete the sentences.

1 Oxfam helps _victims_ of famine and other disasters.

2 When there is a _____, a lot of water covers the land.

3 Scientists are trying to find _____ to the problem of pollution.

4 When there is a _____, the wind can pull off the roofs of houses.

5 Floods and earthquakes are natural _____.

6 A _____ happens when there is not enough food in a country.

7 My aunt works for a _____. They collect money for ill children.

8 When houses are destroyed in a flood, people have no _____.

9 There are poor people in all countries. Sadly, _____ is a global problem.

10 Our school sold cakes to _____ money for charity.

Reading comprehension

4 Write *True* or *False*.

1 Oxfam started 100 years ago.   <u>False</u>

2 At first, Oxfam had another name.   _____

3 Oxfam works in lots of countries.   _____

4 Oxfam doesn't try to help people when there are floods.   _____

5 You can sell cakes to help Oxfam.   _____

6 You can pay for a new water tank in a poor village.   _____

7 Oxfam is going to have a website next year.   _____

8 It's important to tell people what you think.   _____

5 Circle the correct words to make true sentences.

1 Oxfam wants to make people's (lives)/ *jobs* better.

2 When it began, Oxfam wanted to help victims of *floods / famine*.

3 In some places, Oxfam trains *health workers / police officers*.

4 Oxfam builds *shopping centres / schools* in some countries.

5 Oxfam makes sure people have clean *homes / water*.

6 You can organize *football matches / exams* to raise money for Oxfam.

7 We can learn more about our world from *newspapers / computer games*.

8 The *Oxford / Oxfam* website can tell you how to help people.

6 Match the two parts of the sentences.

1 Oxfam is   a people who are hungry.

2 Oxfam helps   b has built schools.

3 When there are natural disasters,   c your friend will get a card.

4 In some places, Oxfam   d we can make a better world.

5 You can do lots of things   e a very large charity.

6 If you buy your friend an Oxfam gift,   f Oxfam tries to help.

7 Then Oxfam will send the gift   g to people in a poor country.

8 If we all work together,   h to raise money for Oxfam.

7 Discuss these questions with a partner or with your class.

1 Do you think Oxfam is a good organization? Why or why not?

2 What charities are there in your country? How do they help people?

3 How do you try to help other people?

Writing

More words: Charity work, page 54

GIRLS RAISE MONEY FOR HOSPITAL

Kent schoolgirls Lily and Poppy Brook have collected £80 for their local hospital. Last month, their brother Olly's life was saved by the hospital's emergency team after he was in a bike accident. The girls decided to say 'thank you' by raising money for new equipment at the hospital.

They put on fancy dress costumes to get people's attention and asked them to donate money. They collected £80 in only one hour! Lily and Poppy now want to do more. They plan to have a collection at school next month. 'We want to make sure the hospital continues to save lives,' said Lily.

When you write a news report ...

• Write a short headline in the present tense. Don't use *the* or *a*.

GIRLS RAISE MONEY FOR HOSPITAL

• When you describe people, you can put information before their names:

Kent schoolgirls Lily and Poppy ...

• Use quotes to make the report more interesting:

'We want to make sure the hospital ...'

---

8 Change these sentences into news report sentences. Put information before peoples' names.

1 Sita Patel, who is a teenager from London, raised £250.

2 Ivan Zukov, who is a doctor working at the Manchester Hospital, saved her life.

3 Mary Connolly, who is an ambulance driver from Belfast, was first to arrive.

4 Mr and Mrs Parsons, who are tourists visiting from Canada, saw the accident.

9 Write a newspaper report. Use the information below.

LONDON SCHOOLBOY SELLS PAINTINGS FOR FLOOD VICTIMS

Name	Jack Walters (aged 14)	**Quote**	"I was going to sell my paintings for £1 each, but people wanted to pay more. One man paid £100 for a painting."
Sold	his paintings		
Raised	over £400		
Disaster	flood in Thailand		

Reading

Before reading

1 Discuss these questions.

    1   Where do you think chocolate comes from?

    2   Do you think chocolate is good for you?

    3   Do you prefer eating or drinking chocolate?

2 ‑08‑ Read and listen.

Chocolate

Would you like a piece of chocolate? Most of us enjoy a bar of chocolate – or we like the taste of chocolate in cakes or ice cream. However, not many of us know the history of chocolate. Let's look back in time …

People first made chocolate 3,000 years ago, in Central America and Mexico. They grew cacao trees and used the beans from the trees to make chocolate. The Aztecs used cacao beans as money, because there were no coins or banknotes then. A turkey cost 100 cacao beans and a piece of fruit cost three beans.

At first, people only used chocolate to make a drink. They called the drink *xocolatl*. This means 'bitter water' in an Aztec language because cacao beans have a very bitter taste on their own. Later, people used chocolate as an ingredient in various dishes. They believed that chocolate was good for you, so they used chocolate to treat some illnesses. They also learnt that chocolate will give you energy if you are tired.

During the 16th century, Spanish people travelled to Mexico and were introduced to chocolate. They took chocolate home with them and soon people in Europe started to use chocolate, too. At first, only rich people could enjoy chocolate, because it was very expensive.

In England, people visited special chocolate shops to drink chocolate drinks. They found out that if you add vanilla and sugar to chocolate, it tastes a lot nicer. In about 1690, a doctor called Hans Sloane made a new drink with chocolate and milk. This drink was sweet and tasty, so it was very popular.

Today, chocolate is one of the most popular foods in the world. There are hundreds of different chocolate bars and sweets. We give chocolate as gifts on special occasions. A special treat is chocolate fondue. We heat the chocolate until it melts and then dip fruit into the chocolate. Strawberries are delicious when they are covered in melted chocolate.

There are different kinds of chocolate: dark chocolate, milk chocolate and white chocolate. If you like chocolate, you will be pleased to know that dark chocolate can be healthy. Unlike milk chocolate, dark chocolate does not have a lot of milk and sugar in it. Dark chocolate is good for your heart and helps your blood to move around your body. Eating a small amount of dark chocolate every day can even help protect you from some illnesses.

Vocabulary

3 Match the words from the text to the definitions.

1 <u>blood</u>   *(noun)* the red liquid inside your body

2 _____   *(noun)* the part of your body that makes your blood go round

3 _____   *(verb)* to use medicine to make a sick person well again

4 _____   *(adjective)* having the taste of sugar

5 _____   *(adjective)* having a sharp, unpleasant taste

6 _____   *(adjective)* nice to eat

7 _____   *(noun)* the tree that gives us seeds to make chocolate

8 _____   *(verb)* to put something into a liquid and take it out again

9 _____   *(noun)* a plant that gives a taste to some sweet foods

10 _____   *(verb)* to get warmer and become liquid

Reading comprehension

4 Write *True* or *False*.

1 Long ago, people used cacao beans as money.   <u>True</u>

2 Cacao beans have a very sweet taste.   _____

3 People learnt that you get tired if you drink chocolate.   _____

4 English people took chocolate to Europe.   _____

5 Chocolate wasn't cheap in the 16th century.   _____

6 There were special chocolate shops in England.   _____

7 Milk chocolate is healthier than dark chocolate.   _____

8 A small amount of dark chocolate every day is good for you.   _____

5 Answer the questions.

1 Where was chocolate first made? <u>In Central America and Mexico.</u>

2 Why did the Aztecs use cacao beans as money?

3 When did Spanish people travel to Mexico?

4 Where did people in England drink chocolate?

5 Why did they add vanilla and sugar to chocolate?

6 What did Hans Sloane invent in 1690?

7 What are the three differents kinds of chocolate?

8 Why isn't milk chocolate as healthy as dark chocolate?

6 Complete the facts. Write one word in each gap.

1 The Aztec word for chocolate means ' <u>bitter</u> water'.

2 Chocolate comes from the _____ of the cacao tree.

3 In Aztec times, a _____ cost 100 cacao beans.

4 _____ people learnt about chocolate when they went to Mexico.

5 People liked Sloane's new drink because it was _____ and _____.

6 In a chocolate _____, you dip fruit in melted chocolate.

7 Dark chocolate is good for your _____.

8 If you are tired, chocolate gives you _____.

7 Discuss these questions with a partner or with your class.

1 Which facts in the text are the most surprising?

2 What is your favourite kind of chocolate?

3 How often do you eat or drink chocolate?

Writing

More words: Recipes and cooking, page 55

Colourful cupcakes

Ingredients	Instructions
100g flour	1 Heat the oven to 180°C.
100g butter	2 Put eighteen paper cake cases on a baking tray.
100g sugar	3 Mix the butter and sugar in a large bowl.
2 eggs	4 Add the eggs, flour and vanilla. Stir together.
1 tsp vanilla	5 Divide the mixture into the paper cake cases.
225g icing sugar	6 Bake the cakes in the oven for 20–25 minutes.
30ml water	7 Take the cakes out of the oven. Leave them to cool for 30 minutes.
colourful sweets	8 Mix the icing sugar and water in a large bowl to make icing.
	9 Use the icing and sweets to decorate your cakes.

When you write a recipe, use abbreviations for measurements and temperatures:

1 tsp vanilla (= 1 teaspoon of vanilla) **225g icing sugar** (= 225 grams of icing sugar)

30ml milk (= 30 millilitres of milk) **180°C** (= 180 degrees Celsius)

Use imperatives for each instruction:

Mix the butter and sugar in a large bowl. Take the cakes out of the oven.

7 Match the abbreviations to the words.

1	g		a	teaspoon
2	ml		b	centimetre
3	cm		c	Celsius
4	tsp		d	millilitre
5	C		e	gram

8 Write a recipe. Use the notes below.

Chocolate Cookies

150g flour • 100g butter • 125g sugar • 1 egg • 25g milk chocolate • 1 tsp vanilla

1 heat / oven / 180°C
2 mix / butter / sugar / vanilla / bowl
3 cut / chocolate / into small pieces
4 add / chocolate and flour / stir / mixture / carefully
5 drop / spoons / mixture / baking tray
6 then / bake / cookies / oven / twenty minutes

9 Journeys into space

Reading

Before reading

1 Discuss these questions.

    1 Would you like to be an astronaut?

    2 Where have people gone in space?

    3 Which planets have spacecraft visited?

2 •09• Read and listen.

The History of Space Exploration

For thousands of years people have wanted to know more about space. In ancient Babylon people studied the sun and stars. The ancient Egyptians used the stars to tell the time. In 1609, the Italian scientist Galileo was the first person to study the moon and stars through a telescope. But when did people actually begin to explore space?

Space exploration might not have been possible without an ancient Chinese invention: fireworks. The Chinese filled sticks with gunpowder. When they threw the sticks into a fire, the sticks flew into the air and exploded. These were the first rockets.

In 1898, Russian scientist Konstantin Tsiolkovsky said that people could use rockets to travel into space. For the next few decades, scientists all over the world worked on rockets. On October 4th 1957, a Russian team used a rocket to send the first satellite into space. When this trip was successful, they decided to send a dog into space. On November 3rd 1957, a dog called Laika became the first living creature to travel into space. Sadly, Laika died before the rocket returned to Earth. On August 19th 1960, Russian scientists sent two more dogs, Belka and Strelka, into space on the spacecraft Sputnik 5. This time, the dogs returned to Earth safely.

On April 12th 1961, Russian cosmonaut Yuri Gargarin became the first human to go into space. Eight years later, on July 20th 1969, people all over the world turned on their televisions to see American astronaut Neil Armstrong become the first human to walk on the surface of the moon.

Since then, there have been many exciting developments in space exploration. On December 15th 1970, Venera 7 became the first spacecraft to land on another planet. The Russian spacecraft travelled to Venus and sent information about the planet back to Earth. In 1997 the American spacecraft Pathfinder landed on Mars. A small robot came out of the spacecraft, explored the surface of Mars, and sent some amazing pictures back to Earth.

In the future, perhaps astronauts will not be the only people to travel into space. Some companies already offer flights into space for space tourists. At the moment, these flights cost millions of dollars, so only very rich people can afford them. However, space companies hope that more people will be able to have holidays in space in the future. Perhaps you will visit other planets one day, and look at Earth from space.

Vocabulary

3 Use the words from the text to complete the sentences.

1   In many countries, you can see fantastic _fireworks_ on New Year's Eve.

2   The invention of computers was an important _____ in the 20th century.

3   Russian atronauts are usually called _____s.

4   _____ is dangerous because it causes explosions.

5   Laika's trip was not _____ because she died.

6   The first _____ to land on Venus was called Venera 7.

7   "When did Pathfinder _____ on Mars?" – "In 1997."

8   The _____ of the moon is dry and rocky.

9   _____s in space send television pictures back to Earth.

10 Scientists _____ the jungle to find new plants and animals.

Reading comprehension

4 Number the events in the correct order.

The Russians sent the first satellite into space. ____

A spacecraft landed on Venus. ____

The first human travelled into space. ____

The Chinese invented fireworks. __1__

Sputnik 5 was sent into space. ____

Neil Armstrong walked on the moon. ____

A spacecraft landed on Mars. ____

The first dog travelled into space. ____

5 Correct the information in **bold**.

a telescope

1 Galileo used ~~stars~~ to study the moon.

2 The **Russians** were the first to use rockets.

3 The **Americans** sent the first satellite into space.

4 Laika was the first **astronaut** to travel into space.

5 Yuri Gagarin was the first man **on the moon**.

6 Venera 7 was the first spacecraft to visit **Mars**.

7 You can travel into space for **hundreds** of dollars.

8 Maybe one day we will visit **the sun**.

6 Complete the facts. Write one word in each gap.

1 Galileo was a _____ who lived in Italy.

2 Fireworks were invented by the _____.

3 The first living creature to travel into space was a _____ called Laika.

4 Yuri Gargarin was the _____ man to travel into space.

5 Human beings landed on the _____ in 1969.

6 The first spacecraft to land on _____ was called Venera 7.

7 A small _____ took pictures of Mars.

8 If you want to have a _____ into space, it will cost you a lot of money.

7 Discuss these questions with a partner or with your class.

1 Would you like to travel into space as a tourist?

2 Do you think space tourism will be popular? Why or why not?

Writing

More words: *Space exploration, page 55*

SPACE QUIZ

1 Which is the smallest planet in our solar system?
(It ends with Y.)

2 Which planet is furthest from the Sun? (It starts with N.)

3 What was the name of the first dog to travel in space?

4 How many dogs travelled in Sputnik 5?

5 Who was the first man on the moon?
(His initials are N.A.)

6 When did Yuri Gagarin become the first human to go into space –
1981 or 1961?

7 How far is the moon from Earth – 844,000 km or 8,400 km?

8 What was the name of the spacecraft that sent pictures of Mars
back to Earth? (It begins with P.)

Answers 1 Mercury 2 Neptune 3 Laika 4 Two 5 Neil Armstrong 6 1961
7 About 844,000 kilometres 8 Pathfinder

When you write quiz questions, use a variety of question words:
Who ...   What ...   When ...   Which ...   How many ...   How far ...
Add clues to make questions easier:
It begins with N.   It ends with W.   It's got three letters.

8 Match the clues and the answers.

   1 It begins with S.   a Laika

   2 It ends with A.   b Mercury

   3 It's got four letters.   c Sputnik 5

   4 His initials are Y.G.   d Yuri Gagarin

   5 It's got seven letters.   e Mars

9 Write questions for a quiz about space or a different
subject you know a lot about.

10 It's time for a story

Reading

Before reading

1 Discuss these questions.

    1 Do you like listening to stories?

    2 What are some of your favourite stories?

    3 Do you prefer real stories or imaginary stories?

2 ◄10► Read and listen.

Double Trouble

Kallu and his wife Zahra lived in a little hut on the side of a hill. They were very poor and they didn't have money for food or clothes. They decided to grow some vegetables and sell them at the market, but they didn't have enough money to buy seeds or a spade. They only had Zahra's gold necklace.

Zahra took off her necklace and gave it to Kallu. There were tears in her eyes.

"Sell my necklace at the market," she said. "You can use the money to buy the things we need."

So Kallu sold the necklace and bought some seeds and a spade. He came home and started to work. While he was digging, his spade hit something in the ground. It was a large pot. While Kallu was looking into the pot, a coin fell out of his pocket and landed in the pot. When Kallu tried to take his coin out of the pot, he couldn't believe his eyes. There were now two coins in the pot.

Kallu called Zahra and showed her the pot.

"We're going to be rich," said Zahra happily.

Zahra and Kallu put all their coins in the pot. Soon they had a small pile of coins. Zahra jumped for joy.

"Go and buy my necklace back," she told Kallu. "Buy us some food and new clothes, too."

Kallu went back to the market. He ran as fast as he could. While he was away, Zahra put a potato into the pot, then two potatoes, then four. When Kallu came home, Zahra was sitting on a huge pile of potatoes. When she saw Kallu, she tried to climb down to greet him, but she slipped and fell into the pot. Kallu tried to pull her out, but he fell into the pot too. When Kallu and Zahra climbed out of the pot, another Kallu and another Zahra climbed out.

"Oh no!" said Kallu. "Now there are two Kallus and two Zahras. What are we going to do?"

Kallu scratched his head, but Zahra had an idea.

"Let's build a hut like ours for our new friends," she said. "We'll make them a copy of everything in our hut."

So Kallu built another hut on the other side of the hill. Then he and Zahra put all of their things into the pot, so that the second Kallu and Zahra had everything they needed. The two couples became friends. They weren't rich, but they were happy. Zahra told Kallu to bury the pot deep in the ground.

"That's a good idea," said Kallu. He smiled at Zahra and after that they were never greedy again.

Vocabulary

3 Match the words from the text to the definitions.

1 <u>greedy</u>   (*adjective*) wanting more of things than you really need

2 _____ (*noun*) a tool that you use for digging in the ground

3 _____ (*verb*) to put something in the ground

4 _____ (*noun*) a deep, round container for cooking or storing

5 _____ (*noun*) a lot of things on top of one another

6 _____ (*noun*) to say hello when you see someone

7 _____ (*verb*) to move quickly over something and almost fall

8 _____ (*noun*) a small, simple building with one room

9 _____ (*noun*) a thing that is just like another thing

10 _____ (*noun*) a man and woman who are married

Reading comprehension

4 Write *Kallu* or *Zahra*.

1 <u>Zahra</u> and her husband were very poor.

2 _____ decided to sell her necklace.

3 _____ found a pot in the ground.

4 _____ dropped a coin into the pot.

5 _____ wanted some new clothes.

6 _____ was the first person to fall into the pot.

7 _____ decided to build a hut for their friends.

8 _____ buried the pot in the ground again.

5 Circle the correct words to make true sentences.

1 Kallu and Zahra's *farm* / (*hut*) was on the side of a hill.

2 They wanted to grow vegetables but they didn't have a *spade* / *potato*.

3 Zahra's necklace was made of *gold* / *money*.

4 Kallu's *spade* / *coin* fell into the pot.

5 While Kallu was at the market, Zahra put a *potato* / *coin* in the pot.

6 Kallu fell in the pot when he tried to *take a potato out* / *pull Zahra out*.

7 At the end of the story there were two *children* / *couples*.

8 They were *rich* / *happy* at the end of the story.

6 Write short answers.

1 Were Kallu and Zahra rich at the beginning of the story? <u>No, they weren't.</u>

2 Did they live in a big house? _____

3 Was Zahra's necklace made of gold? _____

4 Did Zahra and Kallu put some money in the pot? _____

5 Did Zahra go to the market with Kallu? _____

6 Were Kallu and Zahra happy at the end of the story? _____

7 Discuss these questions with a partner or with your class.

1 Did you enjoy the story?

2 What lesson did Kallu and Zahra learn?

3 Can you think of a different ending for the story?

4 Do you know any other stories that teach us lessons? What lessons have you learnt from stories you have read?

Writing

More words: Expressing feelings, page 56

A Lucky Day

It was Saturday afternoon. Katie and Sam were in a café, but they weren't happy. Their favourite singer was in town for a concert, but there were no tickets left.

Just then, Sam saw something under the table. He couldn't believe his eyes: four tickets for the concert!

"We can't keep them, can we?" Sam asked, sadly.

"No, we can't," said Katie. "We must take them to the police station."

Katie and Sam gave the tickets to a police officer and gave him their names and their address. Then they went home.

Later that afternoon, the phone rang. It was a girl from Katie's school.

"My name's Emma," she said. "Thank you for finding my tickets. Two of my friends can't go to the concert now. Would you like to come with me?"

Katie and Sam had a great time at the concert. Sam smiled at Katie. "That was a lucky day, wasn't it?" said Sam.

To express feelings in stories, use adjectives:

John was excited when he first flew in an aeroplane.

You can also use actions or expressions to show people's feelings. This will make your writing more interesting:

Sam smiled at Katie. (= Sam was pleased with Katie.)

Kallu couldn't believe his eyes. (= Kallu was very surprised.)

There were tears in her eyes. (= She was very sad.)

She jumped for joy. (= She was very happy.)

---

8 Match the two pairs of sentences to make part of a story.

1 Bob jumped for joy.
2 There were tears in Sarah's eyes.
3 Sally couldn't believe her eyes.
4 Auntie Alice smiled at Emma.

a All her toys were floating in the air.
b "Look! Two tickets for the big match," he said.
c "That was a lovely day," she said.
d "I can't find my doll," she said.

9 Write a story about someone who finds something. Use adjectives or actions to express people's feelings, and use these questions to help you.

- Who is the main character in the story? What does the main character find? How does the main character feel when he / she finds this thing?

- What happens next? What happens in the end? How does the main character feel at the end of the story?

11 Winners

Reading

Before reading

1 Discuss these questions.

    1 Who is your favourite actor or actress?

    2 What is your favourite film?

    3 Have you ever watched 'The Oscars' (the film award ceremony)?

2 ◄11► Read and listen.

The Oscars

The Academy Awards – or 'Oscars' – are prizes for talented actors, writers and directors for their work in films. The awards are given every year at a special ceremony in Hollywood.

The first Academy Awards ceremony was on May 16th 1929 at the Hollywood Roosevelt Hotel. Tickets to the ceremony cost five dollars and there were fewer than 250 people in the audience. The ceremony only lasted for fifteen minutes and it was not on television or radio. In 1953 the awards were shown on TV for the first time. Now, the ceremonies on television last for four hours, and millions of people around the world watch to see their favourite movie stars receive awards.

The audience is made up of hundreds of glamorous actors, but only a few will be winners. Every Academy Award winner is given a golden statue. The statues are called Oscars. They are made of metal and are in the shape of a knight who is standing on a round film can and holding a sword. Fifty new Oscar statues are made every year.

There are different stories about how the Oscar got its name. Some people say that the director of the Academy gave the statue its name in 1931 because she said that it looked like her cousin Oscar. However, actress Bette Davis said that she called her award Oscar as a joke, because her husband's name was Oscar. Nobody knows which story is correct, but in 1939, the Academy named the award the 'Oscar'.

Most Oscar winners have been adults, but a few have been children. In the past the Academy gave out 'baby' Oscars to child actors, which were half the size of the normal statues.

Now, child actors compete against adults for Best Actor or Actress awards. In 1993, Anna Paquin won an Oscar for her acting in a film called *The Piano*. She was eleven!

The person who has won the most Oscars was Walt Disney, who won twenty-six altogether for his films. And the film with the most Oscars was *Titanic*. In 1997, it won eleven Oscars.

Today, the Academy Awards ceremony is very popular. We look forward to the ceremony each year and we want to know who will win. We love to watch talented actors and directors when they win their prizes and say thank you to the audience. And everyone hopes their favourite film will get an Oscar!

Vocabulary

3 Use the words from the text to complete the sentences.

1 At the Olympics, winners are given medals in a special _ceremony_.

2 Children aren't allowed to drive – only _____ can drive a car.

3 Famous actors are sometimes called _____ _____.

4 In the football World Cup, teams from different countries _____ against each other.

5 Brave soldiers in the past that rode horses were called _____s.

6 My sister's getting married soon, and I'm looking _____ to the wedding.

7 That cake is too big to eat so I'll only eat _____ of it.

8 My brother is never serious. He's always making _____s.

9 That actress with the diamond necklace looks very _____.

10 The Oscars are _____ for actors and other people who make films.

Reading comprehension

4 Circle the correct words to make true sentences.

1 The Oscars are *ceremonies* /(*prizes*) given to people who work in films.

2 The prizes are given at a special ceremony in *New York* / *Hollywood*.

3 The first Oscars ceremony lasted for *five* / *fifteen* minutes.

4 Now *250* / *millions of* people watch the Oscars.

5 The winners are given a small *statue* / *sword*.

6 The statues were called Oscars in *1931* / *1939*.

7 Child actors used to get *adult* / *baby* Oscars.

8 *Titanic* won *eleven* / *twenty-six* Oscars.

5 Number the sentences in the correct order.

The Academy named the awards 'Oscars'.   _____

Anna Paquin, aged 11, won an Oscar.   _____

The first Academy Awards ceremony took place.   _____

The Academy director said the statues looked like her cousin.   _____

Titanic won 11 Oscars.   _____

The Oscars ceremony was on TV for the first time.   _____

The first films were produced.   __1__

6 Match the two parts of the sentences.

1 The Academy Awards are also called   a on television or radio.

2 The Academy Awards   b every year.

3 The first Oscars ceremony wasn't   c Oscars.

4 The first Oscars ceremony took place   d than any other film maker.

5 Fifty new Oscars are made   e in a hotel in Hollywood.

6 No one really knows   f the Oscars ceremony.

7 Walt Disney won more Oscars   g how the Oscar got its name.

8 Lots of people look forward to   h are prizes.

7 Discuss these questions with a partner or with your class.

1 Do you think the Oscars ceremony is a good idea?

2 Can you think of other award ceremonies?

3 Do you think it's a good idea to give awards to people? Why or why not?

Writing

More words: Competitions, page 56

The Winner ✩ ✰

My school has an art competition.
We're painting our favourite things.
My best friend is painting a rainbow,
And I'm painting butterflies' wings.

The winner is given a trophy.
They get a certificate, too.
Do you think that I'll be the winner?
Maybe my wish will come true.

Every year, when the winner is chosen,
There's a ceremony in the school hall.
The art teacher shows the best painting
And then hangs it up on the wall.

When the art teacher held up my painting,
I heard a big cheer from the crowd.
My friends were all laughing and clapping.
I felt very happy and proud.

When you write a poem, remember …

- A poem is usually made of different verses. This one has four. Can you see them?
- We sometimes use rhyming words when we write a poem. For example 'things' and 'wings' in the first verse. Can you find more rhyming words in the other verses?

8 Complete the poem with the words in the box.

~~everyone~~   go   here   mine   prize   win

Our school sports day is lots of fun,
With lots of games for [1] _everyone_ .
Every year, I close my eyes
And wish that I will win a [2] _____.

I wait for my race to begin.
I'm nervous now, I hope I'll [3] _____.
And then I hear the whistle blow –
The race has started, off we [4] _____!

I run towards the finish line.
I want that medal to be [5] _____
I cross the line, my friends all cheer
"Hooray, hooray! The winner's [6] _____!"

9 Write a poem about a day when you felt happy. Divide your poem into different verses and use rhyming words.

12 Remarkable women

Reading

Before reading

1 Discuss these questions.

    1 Can you name any important women in the world now, or from the past?

    2 Have you ever heard of Pocahontas? Who was she?

2 -12- Read and listen.

The real Pocahontas

Most people know the name Pocahontas because a famous cartoon film about her was made in 1995. The film mixes fact and fiction to create an exciting story. The real Pocahontas wasn't like the Pocahontas in the film. However, she was a remarkable woman and she had an amazing life.

Pocahontas was born in America in about 1595. Her father, Powhatan, was the chief of many Native American tribes in the area that is now called Virginia. Pocahontas's real name was Mataoka, but she was given the nickname Pocahontas because she liked to run and play. Pocahontas means 'playful little girl' in the language of her tribe.

In May 1607, Englishmen sailed to Virginia. One of them was John Smith. Some Native Americans saw John Smith. They didn't know if he was a friend or an enemy so they took him to Chief Powhatan. Smith had to lie down on a big, flat rock. The Chief's men picked up huge sticks and wanted to kill Smith. Suddenly Pocahontas ran to Smith and put her head on his. The men could not hit Pocahontas because she was the Chief's daughter. Pocahontas helped Smith to stand up. Chief Powhatan said that he and Smith were now friends, because Pocahontas had saved Smith's life.

The English built a fort in Virginia. Pocahontas often visited the fort. She took food and clothes for the English and they gave her tools for her people. Unfortunately, the Native Americans and the English were not friends for long. They began to fight and Pocahontas was not allowed to visit the fort so often.

In 1613, Pocahontas met an Englishman called John Rolfe. They fell in love and decided to marry. Their marriage helped to bring peace between the English and Chief Powhatan's people. Pocahontas changed her name to Rebecca and she had a son called Thomas.

In 1616, Pocahontas and her family travelled to England. She met the King of England and many other important people. She also met her old friend, John Smith. Pocahontas became famous in England and people were kind to her. Everyone heard the story of how she saved John Smith's life and helped the English and the Native Americans to become friends.

The Rolfe family stayed in England for seven months. When it was time to return to Virginia, Pocahontas became ill and could not make the long journey back to America. Pocahontas died in England in March 1617. She was only twenty-two years old.

Vocabulary

3 Match the words from the text to the definitions.

1 fort_____ (noun) a strong building that was made to protect a place

2 _____ (noun) the opposite of a friend – someone who hates you

3 _____ (noun) something that really happened

4 _____ (noun) stories that somebody writes that are not true

5 _____ (adjective) unusual and surprising in a good way

6 _____ (adjective) fun and childlike

7 _____ (noun) a name that your friends and family sometimes call you instead of your real name

8 _____ (noun) small groups of people who have the same language or customs

9 _____ (noun) the leader or ruler of a tribe

10 _____ (noun) a time when there is no fighting between people or countries

Reading comprehension

4 Number the events in the correct order.

Pocahontas met the King of England. _____

Pocahontas was given the nickname Pocahontas. _____

Pocahontas married the Englishman John Rolfe. _____

Pocahontas was born in about 1595. __1__

Pocahontas died in England in 1617. _____

Pocahontas saved John Smith's life. _____

Pocahontas went to England. _____

Chief Powhatan's men met John Smith. _____

5 Write *True* or *False*.

1 Pocahontas was a Native American girl. __True__

2 Chief Powhatan was the chief of one Native American tribe. _____

3 John Smith was an Englishman. _____

4 Chief Powhatan said that John Smith was his enemy. _____

5 The people in the fort gave Pocahontas food and clothes. _____

6 Pocahontas married an Englishman called Thomas. _____

7 Pocahontas met lots of important people in England. _____

8 The cartoon film about Pocahontas tells the true story of her life. _____

6 Answer the questions.

1 When was the cartoon film *Pocahontas* made? __In 1995.__

2 What was Pocahontas's real name?

3 What does the word *pocahontas* mean?

4 Why did Chief Powhatan and John Smith become friends?

5 Were Chief Powhatan's people and the Englishmen friends for long?

6 Who did Pocahontas meet in 1613?

7 What was Pocahontas's new name?

8 How old was Pocahontas when she died?

7 Discuss these questions with a partner or with your class.

1 Did any parts of the text surprise you? Why?

2 Do you think Pocahontas was brave? Why or why not?

3 Why do you think we know about more remarkable men than women from the past?

Writing

More words: Life stories, page 56

Helen Keller

Helen Keller was born in Alabama, USA on June 27th 1880. When she was a baby, Helen was very ill and her illness left her deaf and blind. Helen's friend, Martha, helped Helen to create a sign language. By the time she was seven, Helen could use more than sixty signs to talk to her family.

In 1886, the Kellers met an amazing teacher called Anne Sullivan. They asked her to teach Helen. Anne used her finger to 'write' words on Helen's hand. The first word Helen learnt was 'water'. Anne spelt the word on Helen's hand while she ran water over Helen's other hand. Soon she was able to go to school, then university. Later, Helen became a famous speaker and writer. She worked hard to make life better for people with disabilities.

When you write the story of someone's life, use time linkers such as:

when, by the time, later, soon, then, finally

When she was a baby, Helen was very ill.

By the time she was seven, Helen could use more than sixty signs to talk to her family.

Can you find more examples?

7 Read and circle the best time linkers.

¹ *Then / When* Amy was eight, she decided to learn the violin. ² *Later / By the time* she was ten, she could play very well. ³ *When / Soon* she was invited to play in the school concert. She practised every day. *By the time / Finally*, the day of the concert arrived. Amy played beautifully and everyone clapped.

8 Write the life story of Florence Nightingale. Use these notes. Remember to use time linkers.

Name
Florence Nightingale

Born
12th May 1820, in Florence (Italy)

Education
was taught by her father

Interests
helping and caring for sick people

Work
1849 – travelled to Europe to study European hospitals
1850 – travelled to Egypt to study nursing
1853 – was in charge of a women's hospital in London
1854 – went to Turkey and improved conditions in hospitals

Nickname
'The Lady of The Lamp', because she worked all day and all night.

More words

1 Giving instructions

Check the words in your dictionary. Then choose the correct words.

| brush | ~~cardboard~~ | decorate | glue. | scissors | sticky tape |

1 Make a frame for a photo with a piece of [1] *brush / (cardboard)*

2 Cover the front of the cardboard with coloured paper. Use [2] *scissors / sticky tape* to stick the coloured paper to the back of the cardboard.

3 Use a [3] *brush / scissors* to spread [4] *glue / cardboard* on the back of your photo. Stick your photo in the middle of the piece of cardboard.

4 Use [5] *sticky tape / scissors* to cut out some paper flowers.

5 [6] *Decorate / Brush* the sides of the frame with the paper flowers. Stick them round your photo.

2 Personalities

Check the words in your dictionary. Then match the two sentences.

| calm | energetic | ~~friendly~~ | honest | organized | patient |

1 Alfie is friendly.   a He never gets tired.
2 John is calm.   b Her bedroom is always tidy.
3 Sarah is patient.   c He doesn't worry about things.
4 Emma is very organized. d He is nice to everyone.
5 Fred is really energetic. e Everything that she says is true.
6 Mary is honest.   f She doesn't hurry to finish things.

3 Describing places

Check the words in your dictionary. Then complete the sentences.

| avalanche | cliff | glacier | ~~peak~~ | pothole | waterfall |

1 Even in summer, there is snow on the _peak_ of that mountain.

2 We saw a beautiful _____ when we were on holiday. The water in the river falls more than 100 metres.

3 I wouldn't like to go down a _____ . I hate being under the ground.

4   A _____ is a frozen river that moves very slowly.

5   When there is an _____, lots of snow suddenly falls from the side of a mountain.

6   Don't go near the edge of the _____! You could fall.

4 Buildings

Check the words in your dictionary. Then choose the correct words.

| balcony | ~~basement~~ | garage | gate | roof | storey |

1   The (basement) / roof is the bottom part of the building. It is under the ground.

2   The stairs in a house go from one storey / gate to the next.

3   The basement / roof is on top of a house. It covers the house.

4   A storey / balcony is a small place outside a window. People can sit there and see the street.

5   The garage / balcony is a small building for cars, next to the house.

6   The roof / gate is a type of door in the wall or fence, in front of a house.

5 Inventions and technology

Check the words in your dictionary. Then complete the predictions.

| holograms | ~~remote control~~ | solar energy |
| virtual reality | network | screen |

1   I think that we will use a <u>remote control</u> to turn the lights on or off.

2   I hope that I will have a computer with a very big _____.

3   Perhaps we will have _____ of famous sculptures, so we can look at them from every side.

4   I imagine that groups of people will be in the same computer _____. I will talk to my friends using my computer all the time.

5   People will use _____ _____. Houses will have machines on the roof to collect energy from the sun.

6   I think people will play _____ _____ football. The other players will be computer images that seem to be all around you and almost real.

6 Sea life

Check the words in your dictionary. Then complete the sentences.

| backbone | breathe | fin | ~~krill~~ | tentacles | Whale |

1 The sea is full of tiny animals that we can't see. They are called _krill_ .
2 Dolphins can't _____ under water. They have to come to the surface for air.
3 A shark has a _____ on its back. You can see it above the surface of the sea.
4 An octopus has eight long _____. It uses them to hold things.
5 The Blue _____ is the biggest animal on Earth.
6 Fish have a line of bones down the middle of their backs called a _____.

7 Charity work

Some words are often used together in collocations. Check the green collocations in your dictionary.

Oxfam helps victims of floods and other disasters.

Oxfam's helpers provide food for people who are hungry.

When people see films of disasters on TV, they want to donate money.

My mum supports charities that help people in Africa.

My friends and I are making cakes and biscuits to raise money for poor people.

Our teacher is organizing a concert to help victims of the hurricanes in America.

Now match the words to make collocations.

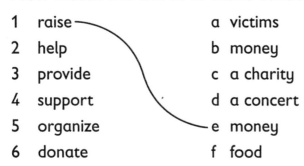

1 raise   a victims
2 help   b money
3 provide   c a charity
4 support   d a concert
5 organize   e money
6 donate   f food

8 Recipes and cooking

Check the words in your dictionary. Then complete the sentences.

| bake | cool | ingredient | ~~mixture~~ | oven | stir |

1 A salad is __mixture__ of cold vegetables – for example, tomatoes, carrots and rice.

2 The most important _____ in a milkshake is milk.

3 When Mum makes soup, she uses a big spoon to _____ it.

4 If you make bread or a cake, you have to _____ it in an oven.

5 The _____ is the part of a cooker that has a door. You bake bread and cakes in it.

6 If food is very hot, you must leave it to _____ before you can eat it.

9 Space exploration

Check the words in your dictionary. Then complete the questions and answers in the Space Quiz.

| atmosphere | comet | galaxy | gravity | ~~orbit~~ | space shuttle |

1 Q: How long does the Earth take to __orbit__ the sun?

   A: It takes one year.

2 Q: When did the first _____ _____ go into space?

   A: On April 12th, 1981.

3 Q: If we went to Mars, could we breathe?

   A: No, we couldn't, because there is no oxygen in the _____ on Mars.

4 Q: What's a _____?

   A: It's something that looks like a star and has a bright tail.

5 Q: What is the word for a very large group of stars and planets?

   A: A _____.

6 Q: Why do rockets need a lot of energy to go into space?

   A: Because _____ pulls everything towards the Earth.

10 Expressing feelings

Read the groups of adjectives. Find the odd-one-out.

1   happy, glad, (sad,) pleased
2   pretty, ugly, beautiful, lovely
3   big, huge, tiny, large

4   nervous, calm, frightened, scared
5   horrible, wonderful, brilliant, great
6   hot, warm, freezing, boiling

11 Competitions

Check the words in your dictionary. Then complete the sentences.

| certificate | competition | loser | ~~medal~~ | race | trophy |

1   At the Olympic Games, the winners get <u>medals</u> made of gold, bronze or silver.
2   The winners of the Football World Cup are given a big gold _____.
3   My friend Nadia is a good runner. She won the _____ last week, but I came second.
4   Every year my school has a _____ to find the best poem.
5   Dad put my _____ in a frame and hung it on the wall.
6   We can't all be winners, so it's OK to be a _____. The important thing is to do your best.

12 Life stories

Check the words in your dictionary. Then match the two parts of the sentences.

| adult | childhood | education | get married | grow up | train (verb) |

1   My grandmother was
2   She grew up
3   She had a loving family, so
4   At the local school she had
5   When she became an adult,
6   She trained to be
7   She met my grandfather in 1964 and they

a   in a small town in Egypt.
b   she went to live in Cairo.
c   got married in 1965.
d   she had a happy childhood.
e   born in 1942.
f   a doctor.
g   a good education.